THE WoW FACTOR

David Wright

ISBN: 978-1-4834-5748-2 (sc)
ISBN: 978-1-4834-5747-5 (e)

Lulu Publishing Services rev. date: 9/27/2016

CONTENTS

EPIGRAPH

This **epigraph** is a literary device in the form of the
following quotation to adopt as a mantra.

Giving Our Best.

Every minute of every day is an opportunity to give our best, to move out of our comfort
zone and be all that we can be.

Be motivated by the wisdom in this book, as you interpret it, that focuses on living and
working each day. The chapters point out that we have experienced yesterday but never
know what tomorrow brings, unless we design our future.

David Wright.

PREFACE

To open….

"In a world of change, the **learners** shall inherit the earth, while the **learned** shall find themselves perfectly suited for a world that no longer exists."

Eric Hoffer
Be a lifelong learner, start here!

David Wright.

OTHER BOOKS BY DAVID WRIGHT

The Health and Safety Mentor.

My first published book was titled "The Health and Safety Mentor." In this book, it is explained that, after 30 years in the Health and Safety profession, I explain everything to the reader in 30 minutes, with them gaining full understanding within an hour….

Taking Charge.

My second published book was named "Taking Charge". "Taking Charge" was three years in the planning, three months in the writing and three months in the editing and proofing. "Taking Charge" is a non-profit making book. The book is about the power of mastery over one's emotions, mind, body and feelings.

Available from our Book Shop:

www.davidwrightservices.co.uk

DEDICATION

"If you believe in yourself and have dedication and pride - and never quit,
you'll be a winner. The price of victory is high but so are the rewards".
Paul Bryant.

This book, "The WoW Factor", is dedicated to all readers who crave self-improvement and have the drive to read it, not as empty words that run around the mind, but for those who go the extra mile, learn, practice and improve. I take my hat off to you all.

Readers attempting to find a **motive** in this narrative will not find it; readers attempting to find a **moral** in it will be disappointed; persons attempting to find a **plot** in it will be disenchanted.

You can be right, you can be wrong, "The WoW Factor" can be a good read with no benefit. It can be a hard study with measurable benefits. You may not progress past page 10. If you find benefit or not – you are right.

David Wright.

FOREWORD

Alison said.

As chief proofer and editor of The WoW Factor, I would encourage you to read this book to gain the inspiration, knowledge and confidence to change your life, career and business focus.

You will find many simple but effective ways within these pages, to gain "the WoW Factor" and progress both your personal and career paths.

PROLOGUE OF "THE WOW FACTOR"

My Career High.

One particular high in my career was being invited to Durham University Business School to participate in a free company business review. We worked with a graduate business consultant, who was employed by Coutts, the Queen's bankers, who possessed an abundance of business skills and was very intuitive. He asked compelling, searching questions, to produce a business report that was my first blue print flagship in years.

In conversation he asked me two questions that took me over ten years to answer. Once the answers were adopted my business grew.

Question 1.0   What do potential clients look for? What skill, quality, attraction and feeling could a potential client look at you and say – WoW?

Question 2.0   The Edge: What is it about your business that gives you the WoW edge?

These two questions and, most importantly, the answers, are the silver thread that runs through this book. Compile your answers to the above questions to start your journey to the WoW Factor.

WHO WILL BENEFIT FROM READING THIS BOOK?

Business people, employees and potential employees.

Business people, employees and potential employees will benefit from reading and learning the lessons in this book.

The WoW Factor is a mastery process.

The WoW Factor is a business and individual mastery process, to benefit the entrepreneur, service business or organisation owner; the employee of such a business or organisation, as well as individuals with a desire to improve their employment status – throughout the book we refer to this as "The WoW Process". So, let's be crystal clear:

The WoW Process.

"The WoW Process {referred to as "1" throughout this book} is the mastery process for the benefit of the entrepreneur, the employee and the individual for career advancement".

HOW "THE WOW FACTOR" IS PRESENTED

Availability of the book and products.

The book is available as a published readable copy. In addition, it is also offered as a training course, presented in an elite printed A4 folder. The book and the training course are accompanied by a CD-ROM which has a number of short, sharp motivational and good business practice videos, refer to Chapter 2 for details.

"The WoW Factor" book, training course, CD-ROM and a talking book version are all available from our Book Shop:

www.davidwrightservices.co.uk

For those who complete the readings and learnings in this book, there is a special valuable free bonus – see page 21.

A walk through the book.

The book is presented in 13 chapters. Each chapter has a main body script, with examples of the main themes where possible.

At the end of each chapter there are 2 exercises relating to that particular chapter plus a "challenge" paragraph. The challenge paragraph is a summary of what has already been read and also a tool to encourage continuity.

THE ENCHANTMENT OF READING

People do not read books.

To state that people do not read books must be followed by the question "why?". I love reading if the book is interesting. If the book is boring, you can guess what happens? Welcome to my style.

The power of imagination.

The teachings in this book, "The WoW Factor", are presented to the reader from on board the interstellar spacecraft WoW, a virtual spaceship which is travelling from Earth to the outer reaches of the mind. En-route, we will experience and touch our humanity, connect with our character and fulfil both our business and personal development desires. We will visit places beyond time and space, places of pure potentiality and spirit, whilst experiencing infinite possibilities of achievement and success beyond the imagination. Our mission is simple, it is to establish whether human potential and development is "limited" or "unlimited" and to discover if the WoW Factor is achievable.

Because of the vast mental distance involved, the journey will span the theoretical lifetime of experience of many generations. Apart from the generation which began the journey, and the generation which might end it, most generations will live, die and be reborn on the ship.

So, fasten your safety belts, relax and stand by for the experience of a lifetime.

INTRODUCTION

In the beginning.

It is Thursday morning, 1st January 2015, Happy New Year David? 2015 is a special year for me, 7th June will mark 30 years of running my own businesses and marketing paralegal, occupational health and safety, health and safety law, quality assurance systems and human resource services. I have worked for, and with, hundreds of companies and individuals and have had the privilege and pleasure of working with, and learning from, many top, successful professional business movers and shakers.

Opposing this, I have met many what I term "business vagabonds", both male and female, who milk the very life blood out of their clients and staff. They cheat, lie and are without scruples to earn a pound, all at the expense of others. Needless to say, I did not work for these miscreants for long, but learned from them the valuable lesson of the types of business people to avoid.

There is a common denominator, a gene of success customarily flowing through business achievements, comparable to a gold thread. Many business people have shared their principles with me and now I share them with you in this, my third book.

Welcome to "The WoW Factor".

What is the WoW Factor?

So, what is the WoW Factor? It is the result of change by adoption of best business principles and business experience. It is an expression of the acquired fundamentals of your business that shines like a white light.

Once acquired your business will flourish and you will double your turnover, if you want to, in one year.

As an individual, the teachings within the enlightening pages of the book will define a pathway from being merely proficient, to that of being exceptional, since each one of us has varying circumstances that might preclude us from being exceptional.

While for one person it may just be typical lassitude, for another it is a genuine lack of resources that they might need to overcome in order to arrive at the exceptional place.

Either way, there is no pretext for inaction at the table of exceptional living.

> *"The price of success is hard work, dedication to the job at hand,*
> *and the determination that, whether we win or lose, we have*
> *applied the best of ourselves to the task at hand".*
> *Vince Lombardi.*

Orbiting, stagnant and struggling.

Do you find your business orbiting, stagnant and struggling to develop?

Are you a budding enthusiastic person actively seeking work? Are you an employee in employment, but currently suffering from a lack of intellectual stimulation and wanting to improve yourself and your prospects?

Do you need a little professional help?

By reading, studying and adopting the principles written in the pages of this book, you will learn individual skills and gain enough confidence to take your business, or your job, to the next level and double your turnover or income within one year.

You will come to be a worthy respectable employee or a sort after person, headhunted by the best companies. Does this sound a bit of a fantasy? No, after reading this book, completing all the exercises and, with an open heart and mind, adopting the principles, you, the employer, employee or the individual looking for work, will experience the magic of knowledge, confidence and become an esoteric individual: you will have "it", the WoW Factor.

Completion of the book "The WoW Factor".

This book, "The WoW Factor", after one hard year, was completed on 31st December 2015. In January 2016, we commenced the grammar and technical proofing, editing and critical analysis process of the manuscript's content. The result was a suggestion that, following publication of "The WoW Factor", we should consider reproducing the script as a training course, adding graphics and a supporting DVD containing short and sharp training videos. Accepting this suggestion, this book is now available as a bound book and as a training course presented in an A4 folder, sold and distributed via our website. The purchaser of "The WoW Factor" Book or Training Package can have, with our compliments, a free consultation session with the author or a group associate.

Visit our Book Shop:

www.davidwrightservices.co.uk
and email the author.

Business in crisis.

In the beginning, organisations and companies purchased services on a "need" basis. With the introduction of price comparison websites and competitive tenders, they then purchased services based on "price" or "cost".

"Cheap goes with nasty as nasty goes with cheap".

The service industry was flooded with second class services and business was in crisis. Business practices needed to change if they were going to survive. Introduction of quality assurance, particularly ISO 9001: 2007 now 2015, provide a professional standard of business competence.

Business has a new paradigm, a distinct set of concepts for the service industry. The distinctive pinnacle of the new paradigm is:

"Companies purchased services based on confidence and not cost."

Rather than focus on why there is a crisis, focus on business resurrection and resolution which are one and the same imposter.

*"The Chinese use two brush strokes to write the word 'crisis.' One
brush stroke stands for danger; the other for opportunity. In a crisis,
be aware of the danger, but recognise the opportunity."*
John F. Kennedy.

Resolution of the hidden crisis.

Resolve the business crisis as fast as possible, as this will provide damage control and protect reputation. The longer this latent crisis is left unattended, the more it will disrupt daily business operations. Your mission to enter the WoW Factor is to get to the next business platform or employment status level.

The Intrapreneurship.

As an Intrapreneurship – by definition this is the act of behaving like an entrepreneur whilst working within a large organisation. Intrapreneurship is known as the practice of a corporate management style that integrates risk-taking and innovative approaches, as well as the reward and motivational techniques that are more traditionally regarded as being the province of entrepreneurship.

The purpose of this book.

The purpose of this book is twofold:

Purpose 1: "Change Management" – "Change Management" is a comprehensive term used to describe change at both individual and organisational level.

For example, the term "Change Management" is used to describe:

Task	The task of managing change;
Professional Practice:	An area of professional practice;
Knowledge:	A body of knowledge {consisting of models, methods, techniques and other tools}; and
Control:	A control mechanism {consisting of requirements, standards, processes and procedures}.

Change management is also used to describe the process following the change in manufacturing services or present thinking. Also computerised systems, logging best practices or system upgrades, for example, my focus in this book is to define change management, with the counsel of the business gurus, as it relates to people's experience and the organisational process. Then add a little "WoW".

Purpose 2: "The WoW Factor" - What is the WoW Factor? "Wow" is a transitive verb used to express amazement, great pleasure and wonderment in acknowledgment of your great success. "Factor" is a part that actually contributes to an accomplishment, result or process.

"Surprise is the greatest factor of war."
Tom Clancy.

Interstellar spacecraft WoW, departing to Chapter 1 "The Clear Focus".

"….Please take your seats and fasten your seat belts.

Welcome on board the interstellar spacecraft WoW, a virtual spaceship which is travelling from Earth to the outer reaches of the mind.

We will be departing in 5 minutes, we will be travelling at the speed of light and will arrive at Chapter 1 "The Clear Focus" in around 9 minutes…."

CHAPTER 1

Interstellar spacecraft WoW has arrived at....

The Clear Focus

"What you focus on magnifies"
"The clear focus is clear, sharp, distinct, crisp and sharp-edged"

Before commencing your journey through Chapter 1 "The Clear Focus", go to page 31 to read about the supporting CD-ROM that accompanies this book.

Welcome back, let's start.

This chapter is the process beginning.

Welcome! We hope you enjoyed your first journey on the spacecraft WoW of imagination. We are currently at the station "here and now", Chapter 1 "The Clear Focus", and will travel at light speed though a lifetime of folk-law, legend, bad habits and hope, eventually arriving at the end of "The WoW Factor" book, through time, to a place of infinite possibilities, meeting the "You Unlimited Company".

We start our journey to the WoW Factor. The first stop is "The Clear Focus". You will be taking notes and progressing through a number of exercises on your journey to the WoW Factor, so make sure you have a hard-back journal and pencil before we commence Chapter 1.

Chapter 1 "The Clear Focus" is about:

1.1   Learning from others.
1.2   The WoW Factor - meaning.

1.1 Learning from others: In my 30 years of operating my occupational health and safety, hygiene and risk management practice, I have been an analytical chemist, a paralegal practitioner, a process server, an accident claims and fraud investigator, a quality assurance consultant, a private investigator, a human resources advisor and now a published author.

In my spare time I have been a neuro-linguistic programme {NLP} practitioner, a life coach, a hypnotist and a motivational speaker. When I say that I have "been" in these professions, I have also qualified in them and earned professional fees from them.

My point is that the silver thread running through my 30 year career, is that I have met, at seminars {both presented and attended}, worked for, worked with and spoken to, perhaps thousands of professionals every day, pleasant and, on occasion, ghastly men and women. Considering the multitudes, the majority I liked, the minority I disliked and a few I really admired.

The important point being, I intellectually inherited from a few the mastered art of successful business management, by listening, learning and comparing.

"People have shared with me, now I share with you".

1.2 The WoW Factor - meaning: The "WoW Factor" is a term that is a response from your client, or potential client, when expressing their amazement, great pleasure and wonderment in acknowledgment after meeting you, hearing your business proposals and in response to the finished job – WoW!

Contrary to "WoW" is the "dislike determinant" - meaning the dark side of the "WoW Factor" equation. With the "dislike determinant", your client, or potential client, does not like the way you look, what you say, the way you say it, what you promise and has no confidence in either you or your service.

Every journey starts with a first step and the first step to the WoW Factor is a clear focus – your personal laser of yourself – your appearance, what you say and how you verbally present yourself.

Your business laser is your focus in understanding and adopting an approach on how you conduct the day-to-day management of your business. The impression I gain purely by the fact that you are reading this book, is that you could be a one-person service business, either self-employed or a limited liability, or you could be in a partnership, or even a Limited Liability Partnership {LLP}. Alternatively, you could be a section or departmental "head" in a large company or organisation. Regardless of the classification of reader, you can gain quantifiable benefit by understanding and adopting the principles in this book.

"The WoW Factor".

You have two chances to make a first impression, viz – what you look like and what you say.

1.3   The Clear Focus:

How you present yourself – how you look {your appearance}.

The Clear Focus is the first step towards entering "The WoW Factor". The Clear Focus is in two sections:

- How you present yourself – how you look {your appearance}.
- How you project your business.

How you present yourself – how you look {your appearance}. Successful businessmen and women look the part, say the right things, do what they say and are masters at listening. Let me explain:

Looking the part means that you look like you belong doing what you are doing. A bank executive would be well groomed and dressed in a decent business suit. A painter would probably be wearing something that can be washed easily, like a uniform, coveralls or bib and brace overalls. A beautician would probably have the latest hair style and wear elaborate make-up.

Dressing correctly for work is essential. Imagine attending a meeting at the bank and the bank executive is wearing a track-suit and trainers, what would be your first impression?

A painter arrives on your doorstep to provide you with a quote to paint your house wearing raggy overalls, covered in paint splatters, what would be your first impression? Finally, the beautician is dressed in shorts and slippers, what would be your first impression? The choice is yours viz the "WoW Factor" image or the "dislike determinant". So, you meet a potential client or an existing client looking like a "new-age traveller" or as if you are on your way to the gym instead of projecting the image of a professional person, which roads do you think you are going down? It has always amazed me that a lot of business professionals do not dress correctly.

1.4   **Exercise 1: Image Dressing:** Image is the general impression that a person projects to the public. For this exercise, list the circumstances, venues and reasons that you come into contact with your clients and/or potential clients. Then describe your mode of dress. Do not just "think" this exercise – write it down and do it!

This exercise changed my business image. If after meeting delegates they cannot remember my name, they refer to me as the….

"immaculately smart one with shiny shoes".

To continue, the next part of presenting yourself, after appearance, is "what" you say and "how" you say it. When talking to your clients and/or potential clients, here are my top guideline points on the skill of conversing with them:

1.   Speak quietly and slowly, do not raise your voice or shout. Be natural, practice fairly slow monologue in front of a mirror, using a newspaper or similar. Another good idea is to record a prose into a recording device, i.e. your iPhone. Practice, practice, and practice some more, because repeated practice leads to mastery.
2.   Remove from your vocabulary words and phrases such as "didn't we" and "isn't it" etc. Such words and phrases are "yes tags" and are habitually calling for the other person to say "yes".
3.   Practice listening skills. A good conversation is 40% talking, 40% listening and 20% gentle silence.

The next part of "what" you say and "how" you say it is to say the right things. What do I mean? I mean when talking to clients and/or potential clients regarding current contracts or potential contracts.

Remember, these people are not your friends; they are the people who look at you to provide a professional service. When conversing, you need to instil confidence by expressing your understanding of what they want, as well as your knowledge and experience to provide it. So, be able to explain yourself clearly, distinctly and succinctly.

Do what you say. Never exaggerate or make claims or promises that you cannot fulfil. Finally, master the art of listening. Listening involves not interrupting, hearing the spoken words and then interpreting the spoken words.

1.5   Exercise 2: Speaking and Listening: You have a meeting with a potential new client. Write a script, detailing your conversation with him.

Write your introduction viz:

"I'm John Brown, the Principal of the Practice......" followed by the details of the proposed contract, *viz – "from our initial conversation I understand....",* followed by your proposal, viz – *"what I propose, Mr Brown, is...."* and, finally, the closing, viz – *"well Mr Brown, it was a pleasure to meet you, is there anything you want to ask me ????, I will compile a proposal for you and you will receive it next Wednesday, is that acceptable? ......"*

1.6   The Challenge: Here we are at the end of the first chapter of "The WoW Factor".

The challenge is for you to complete the two exercises, before you continue your journey to the WoW Factor.

Interstellar spacecraft WoW, departing from Chapter 1 "The Clear Focus" and heading to Chapter 2 "Supporting CD-ROM"

"….Please take your seats and fasten your seat belts.

We will be departing in 5 minutes from Chapter 1 "The Clear Focus", we will be travelling at the speed of light and will arrive at Chapter 2 "Supporting CD-ROM" in about 3 minutes…."

CHAPTER 2

Interstellar spacecraft WoW has arrived at....

Supporting CD-ROM

"You will treasure these short films"

"The WoW Factor" is available in book format and also as a training course presented in a personalised A4 Folder. To support your reading and/or studying we have compiled 12 videos. If you purchased the book or folder from our website, we will have included the CD-ROM with your purchases, however, if you purchased your book or folder from a bookshop or Amazon, please contact the author and we will send you a copy of the CD-ROM by return.

Visit our Book Shop:

www.davidwrightservices.co.uk
and email the author.

Accompanying your copy of "The WoW Factor" is a CD-ROM.

Index of CD-ROM contents:

1.0   Customer Service:

- Understanding Customer Needs.
- Business Goals.
- Decision Criteria.
- Personal Goals.

2.0 How to create loyal customers:

Fact - it costs five times more to acquire a new customer than to keep a current one.

3.0 Loyalty Expert: Fred Reichheld:

How to achieve extraordinary results with the net promoter management system.

4.0 Action Centred Leadership:

Performing the Task: Maintaining the Team and Supporting the Individuals.

5.0 Ten Leadership Theories in Five Minutes – {Professor Michael Zigarell}:

The Great Man Theory.
The Trait Theory of Leadership.
The Skills Theory of Leadership.
The Leadership Style.
The Situational Leadership Theory.

6.0 Andrew Roberts: Churchill: Secrets of Leadership:

The London Business School. A talk about how Winston Churchill inspired the nation to win the Second World War.

7.0 Scott Geller: The Psychology of self-motivation:

Presentation by TEDx Virginia Tech.

8.0 Mark Bowden: Body Language Expert:

The importance of being authentic.

9.0   Dan Gilbert: Why we make bad decisions:

How to do exactly the right thing at all times, or the idea that changed the World.

10.0 McKinsey on change management:

70% of change programmes fail.

11.0 Rosabeth Moss Kanter:

Six keys to leading positive change:
11.1   The Universal Lesson of Life - show up.
11.2   It is important to speak up.
11.3   Look up - at some higher principal or issue, vision and values.
11.4   Team up - everything goes better with partners.
11.5   Never give up: Cantor's law stated that everything can look like a failure in the middle.
11.6   Lift others up - share the success and the credit with others.

12.0 Five Character Traits of Top Performers:

There are two types of employee: one who turns up for the cosy cheque and one who turns up to work diligently. The first group notices how slow the minute hand is moving. The second group could not care less about the first group. Why? Because group two are the top performers.

The five characteristics are:
12.1   Knowing your environment.
12.2   Behaviours.
12.3   Mastering your skills.
12.4   Values and Beliefs.
12.5   Identity.

**Interstellar spacecraft WoW, departing from
Chapter 2 "Supporting CD-ROM" and will arrive at
Chapter 3 "Change Management" shortly.**

"….Please take your seats and fasten your seat belts.

We will be departing in 5 minutes from Chapter 2 "Supporting CD-ROM", we will be travelling at the speed of light and will arrive at Chapter 3 "Change Management" in about 3 minutes…."

CHAPTER 3

Interstellar spacecraft WoW will be arriving at....

Change Management

I hope you found your visit to "The Clear Focus" both enlightening and educational. Trusting you to have completed the two exercises contained within "The Clear Focus", it was then back on board the spacecraft WoW of imagination, departing from "The Clear Focus" and travelling at light speed to "Change Management". On the way we stopped at Chapter 2 and learned about the supporting DVD package and how to receive a copy.

We have now arrived - Welcome to "Change Management".

"To be effective, successful and positive - change management should be multi-disciplinary, reaching all aspects of the organisation".

Chapter 3 "Change Management" is about:

3.1   Effective Change Management.
3.2   Complex Change.
3.3   Responsibility for managing change.
3.4   Management principles.
3.5   The Eight Step Change Model.
3.6   Exercise 3: Define one major change you are going to adopt into your business.
3.7   Exercise 4: Define your method of implementation and empower action.
3.8   Exercise 3 and 4, examples.
3.9   The Challenge.

3.1   Effective Change Management:

Change management is the WoW Process[1] of the management of change to move from where you are to where you want to be. The following effective directions will be more successful if you apply these simple principles. In addition, achieving personal change will be more successful if you use the same directional approach, where relevant.

3.1.1   Change management entails thoughtful planning, sensitive implementation and, above all, both consultation with and the involvement of the people affected by the changes. If you force change on people problems usually arise.

3.1.2   Change must be realistic, achievable and measurable. These aspects are especially relevant to managing personal change.

3.1.3   Before starting organisational change, think:

What do we want to achieve with this change?
Why?
Also, how will we know that the change has been achieved?

{"The WoW Process [referred to as "1" throughout this book] is a mastery process for the benefit of the entrepreneur, the employees and the individual to career advancement"}.

Who is affected by this change and how will they react to it?

How much of this change can we achieve ourselves?
Which parts of the change do we need help with?

These aspects relate strongly to the management of personal as well as organisational change.

3.1.4   Do not 'sell' change to people as a way of accelerating agreement and implementation. 'Selling' change to people is not a sustainable strategy for success.

3.1.5   When people listen to a senior management person 'selling' them a change, decent diligent folk will generally smile and appear to accept what is being said, whilst quietly thinking to themselves:

"I don't like this. I've not been consulted or involved. I am being manipulated. This change will benefit the directors and owners, not me, so I will not cooperate and I might even resist and obstruct this change".

3.1.6   Instead, change needs to be understood and managed in a way that people can cope with more effectively. Change can be unsettling, so the manager logically needs to be a settling influence.

3.1.7   Check that people affected by the change agree with, or at least understand, the need for change. Give them the chance to decide how the change will be managed, and the chance to be involved in both the planning and implementation of the change.

3.1.8   Use face-to-face communications to handle sensitive aspects of organisational change management. Encourage your managers to communicate face-to-face with their people if they are helping you to manage an organisational change. Email and written notices are extremely weak at conveying and developing understanding.

3.1.9   If you think that you need to make a change quickly, probe the reasons - is the urgency real? Will the effects of agreeing a more sensible timeframe really be any more detrimental than presiding over a disastrous change?

3.2   Complex Change:

For complex changes, refer to the process of project management, ensuring that you augment this with consultative communications to agree and gain support for the reasons for the change. Involving and informing people also creates opportunities for others to participate in planning and implementing the changes, which lightens your burden and spreads the organisational load, whilst creating a sense of ownership and familiarity among the people affected.

To understand more about people's personalities and how different people react differently to change, refer to paragraph 3.5 "Eight Step Change Model" on page 38.

3.3   Responsibility for managing change:

The employee does not have a responsibility to manage change - the employee's responsibility is nothing more than to do their best, which is different for every person and depends on a wide variety of factors {health, maturity, stability, experience, personality, motivation, etc.}.

The responsibility for managing change lies with the management and executives of the organisation - they must manage the change in a way that employees can cope with.

3.4   Management principles:

3.4.1   At all times involve and agree support from people within the system:

> System = environment, processes, culture, relationships, behaviors, etc., whether personal or organisational.

3.4.2   Understand where you and/or the organisation are at the moment.

3.4.3   Understand where you want to be, along with the when, why and what measures will be needed to get there.

3.4.4   Plan development towards paragraph 3.4.3 above in appropriate achievable measurable stages.

3.4.5   Communicate, involve, enable and facilitate involvement from people, as early, openly and as fully as possible.

3.5   Eight Step Change Model.

Eight step change model can be summarised as:

Step 1:   Increase urgency - inspire people to move, make objectives real and relevant.

Step 2:   Build the guiding team - get the right people in place with the right emotional commitment, as well as the right mix of skills and levels.

Step 3:   Get the vision right - get the team to establish a simple vision and strategy, focus on the emotional and creative aspects necessary to drive service and efficiency.

Step 4: Communicate for "buy-in", involve as many people as possible, communicate the essentials simply, appeal and respond to people's needs. De-clutter communications - make technology work for you rather than against.

Step 5: Empower action - remove obstacles, enable constructive feedback and gain lots of support from leaders - reward and recognise progress and achievements.

Step 6: Create short-term wins - set aims that are easy to achieve in bite-size chunks. Provide manageable numbers of initiatives. Finish current stage before starting new ones.

Step 7: Do not let up - foster and encourage determination and persistence - ongoing change - encourage ongoing progress reporting - highlight achieved and future milestones.

Step 8: Make change stick - reinforce the value of successful change via recruitment, promotion and new change leaders. Weave change into culture.

3.6 Exercise 3: Change Management {1}: Define one major change that you are going to adopt into your business.

3.7 Exercise 4: Change Management {2}: Define your method of implementation and enable action. Define and state how to remove obstacles, enable constructive feedback and gain lots of support from leaders - reward and recognise progress and achievements.

3.8 Exercise 3 and 4, examples:

Exercise 3: Change Management {1}. Define one major change you are going to adopt into your business.

To change the office structure from "Paper" to "Paperless", starting a paperless office to avoid your business drowning in a sea of paper.

Storing all this paper is not the only issue: how do you keep it all properly filed? How can you locate it later when you need it? How do you easily provide a copy to a client or another party?

Considerations before going paperless - There is more to becoming paperless than simply buying a scanner and some software, although these are important pieces in the process and we will discuss their importance a little later. Before you scan your first piece of paper, you need to determine a number of things to establish a process and procedures that can be easily followed by everyone.

Workflow - Once you have made the decision to go paperless and have decided how you will organise your folders and files, you will need to map out your proposed workflow. You will use this workflow chart, along with your decisions on folder and file naming structure, to create a written policy for your office. Remember that implementing a scanning and storage policy is not something that you just want to jump into without prior thought and planning.

Taking it to the next level - If you want to take your scanning and storage to the next level, then use a practice management system such as "Time Matters".

Exercise 4: Change Management {2}. Define your method of implementation and empower action. Define and state how to remove obstacles, enable constructive feedback and gain lots of support from leaders - reward and recognise progress and achievements.

What you need to get started - To begin your move to a paperless office, you only need a few basic tools to get started, as detailed below:

Computer. Computer prices continue to drop and no-one should be using a system that is more than three years old. This is to ensure that your hardware does not create a bottleneck for going paperless.

Scanner. It is understood that you will need one or more scanners in your office. The real question is what type of scanner and what features should it have? Start with a sheet-fed scanner.

PDF software. You must have PDF software to go paperless. The "De Jure" file format for electronic documents in most instances today is PDF {Portable Document Format}.

Backup tools. Moving to a paperless office means that you can now easily back up all of your files and you must do so. A solid backup plan should target all of your critical files and should include both online backup as well as a rotating series of local backups in which the backup media is moved off-site.

3.9 **The Challenge:** Here we are at the end of the third chapter, "Change Management". Time to compose paragraph 3.6 {Exercise 3: Change Management {1}}. You need to define one major change that you are going to adopt into your business.

It is also time to compose paragraph 3.7 {Exercise 4: Change Management {2}}. You will need to define your method of implementation and empower action.

The challenge is extended to review Exercises 1 and 2 at the end of Chapter 1 "The Clear Focus" viz paragraph 1.4 {Exercise 1: Image Dressing} and paragraph 1.5 {Exercise 2: Speaking and Listening}.

See you in Chapter 4 "The Supremacy of Goal Setting".

Interstellar spacecraft WoW, departing from Chapter 3 "Change Management" and will soon arrive at Chapter 4 "The Supremacy of Goal Setting".

"….Please take your seats and fasten your seat belts.

We will be departing in 5 minutes from Chapter 3 "Change Management", travelling at the speed of light and will arrive at Chapter 4 "The Supremacy of Goal Setting" in about 3 minutes…."

CHAPTER 4

Interstellar spacecraft WoW will be arriving at....

The Supremacy of Goal Setting

I hope you found your visits to "The Clear Focus" and "Change Management" both informative and instructive.

On the way, we stopped and arranged for delivery of the supporting CD-ROM package. To review, you should now have four completed exercises in your journal. If you have not, then STOP and go back to Chapter 1.

> *"Have you done your exercises or not? Some people want success but not effort. Other people make the effort to be successful – which type of person are you?"*

> *"This is the Captain speaking - at the speed of light we are approaching our next stop - The Supremacy of Goal Setting".*

Here we are at "The Supremacy of Goal Setting" - so let's begin.

> *"The importance of goals is to increase motivation, by the adoption of a goal setting process".*

Your destiny is in your own hands.

Prologue:

The reason for this preface viz Prologue is to introduce the sub-paragraphs of Chapter 4 "The Supremacy of Goal Setting". This is because of my unwavering belief that the power and understanding of goal setting is the difference between "success" and "failure", depending upon your definitions of the words "success" and "failure".

You must read "The Strangest Secret" by Earl Nightingale. The "secret" is simply six words:

"We become what we think about".

This is certainly no new idea. In fact, Earl Nightingale admits that he learned it from Napoleon Hill's classic book "Think and Grow Rich". In that book it also stated that this was not a unique idea. There are an abundance of other books that have expanded on the concept, such as Marc Allen's "The Millionaire Course" or James Allen's "As a Man Thinketh" {later retitled to "As You Think"}. To apply the "we become what we think about" philosophy in personal goal setting, by thinking one has already achieved the possibility of goal success quadruples the likelihood of success.

Read Chapter 4 "The Supremacy of Goal Setting" over and over again to lock in the principles, practices and models of goal setting, you will have one foot firmly on the WoW Factor treadmill.

Goal setting works.

Chapter 4 "The Supremacy of Goal Setting" is about:

4.1   What is Goal Setting?
4.2   A Goal Setting Action Plan.
4.3   Concept.
4.4   Exercise 5: Listing.
4.5   Exercise 6: Goal Notation.
4.6   The Challenge.

4.1   What is Goal Setting?

Goal setting involves the development of an action plan, {refer to paragraph 4.2 below}, designed to motivate and guide a person or a group towards a goal.

Goal setting is a major component of personal development and management improvement.

4.2 A Goal Setting Action Plan:

Goal setting action plans are used widely by top-level business people, high achievers and people from all levels of society. The Goal Setting Action Plan can also be a more formal process for career and personal planning. The goal setting action plan process of setting goals and targets allows you to categorise your goal into clusters:

"Your goals - what would you like to "Be", "Do" and "Have"."

Business Goals: How do you see {desire} your business to "Be" and "Look" in 1 year, 3 years' and 5 years' time? Under each timeline there are six sub-headings:

1. Scope of operations goals.
2. Premises goals.
3. Staffing goals.
4. Turnover goals.
5. Management team goals.
6. Personal goals.

What do you want for yourself?

1. Health goals.
2. Personal wealth goals.
3. Educational goals.
4. Social goals.
5. Five things you want goals.

Financial Goals: It could be that you are yearning to have zero credit card debt, you have been invited by friends to join them for an "away" weekend but have no idea how you to are going to pay for the trip, or you have a long-term ambition to put your two-year-old through college someday.

Setting financial goals is one step towards creating your dream life.

1. Set up a rainy day fund goal.
2. Find an investment advisor goal.
3. Evaluate your financial situation goal.
4. Eliminate bad debt goal.
5. Consolidate savings and bank account goal.

Family Goals: To realise our dreams, goals and aspirations, both as a family and as individuals, in a way that stretches our intellect, supplements our faith, strengthens our character and enriches our family life. So that we are fulfilled, happy, confident and always close.

1.   Create a Family Mission Statement goal.
2.   To live in the house of your dreams goal.
3.   To give a little back to the community goal.
4.   To appreciate friends goal.
5.   To do the things we enjoy goal.

4.3   Concept:

Goals that are deemed difficult to achieve tend to increase performance more than goals that are not. A goal can become more specific through quantification or enumeration {should be measurable}, such as by demanding an increase in productivity by 50%, or by defining certain tasks that must be completed.

Setting goals affects outcomes in four ways:

-   **Choice:** Goals separate beneficial choices from counter-productive choices.
-   **Effort:** If you are focused on a goal, the white noise of life becomes less distracting and you are able to put more energy into your goal.
-   **Persistence:** Goals provide known "outcomes". Knowing an outcome will add extra drive to sometimes arduous tasks leading to one's goal.
-   **Cognition:** Goals allow you to plan and then make changes in yourself that you may not otherwise be compelled to make.

Motivate yourself to achievement, it gives you long-term vision and short-term motivation. It focuses your acquisition of knowledge and helps you to organise your resources.

-   Define the objects.
-   Stay focused on your objective.
-   Decide what is important for you to achieve in your life and start, step-by-step, achieving these goals.
-   Track and record your progress and achievements.

Increase your self-confidence as you develop your level of competence in achieving your goals. This is very important, as self-confidence is critically important during the job searching process and many organisations place a high value on this quality.

4.4   **Exercise 5: Listing:** List 20 goals under the three headings {Business, Financial and Family} above. The secret is to write the three individual headings then add the six sub-headings under each section. Then write for 10 minutes, use your imagination, focus on the heading and let your pen do the work.

4.5   **Exercise 6: Goal Notation:** You now have a written "goal notation". Now, for each goal, mark a "timeline" of achievement, viz: 1 month, 6 months, 12 months, 18 months and 2 years. Now, for each "timeline" add two review dates. Finally, print out the "goal notation" and for each goal write "why" you want to achieve success.

Remember: The "why" is the driving force behind human behaviour. Find a big enough "why" and the "how" will follow. Imagine you have already achieved the individual goal.

Remember: We become what we think about.

4.6   **The Challenge:** Here we are at the end of Chapter 4 "The Supremacy of Goal Setting". It is now time for the exercises. Complete Exercise 5 by writing 20 goals under the 3 headings. Then continue and complete Exercise 6, for each goal mark a "timeline" of achievement.

The challenge is extended to review all exercises.

Refer to paragraph 1.4 on page 28 - Exercise 1: Image Dressing: Image is the general impression that a person projects to the public. For this exercise, list the circumstances, venues and reasons that you come into contact with your clients and/or potential clients. Then describe your mode of dress. Do not just "think" this exercise – write it down and do it!

Refer to paragraph 1.5 on page 29 - Exercise 2: Speaking and Listening: You have a meeting with a potential new client. Write a script, detailing your conversation with him. Write your introduction viz – "I'm John Brown, the Principal of the Practice……" followed by the details of the proposed contract, viz – "from our initial conversation I understand….", followed by your proposal, viz – "what I propose, Mr Brown, is…." and finally the closing viz – "well Mr

Brown, it was a pleasure to meet you, is there anything you want to ask me ????, I will compile a proposal and you will receive it next Wednesday, is that acceptable? ......"

***Refer to paragraph 3.6 on page 39** - **Exercise 3: Change Management {1}:** Define one major change that you are going to adopt into your business.*

***Refer to paragraph 3.7 on page 39** - **Exercise 4: Change Management {2}:** Define your method of implementation and empower action. Define and state how to remove obstacles, enable constructive feedback and gain lots of support from leaders - reward and recognise progress and achievements.*

***Refer to paragraph 4.4 on page 47** - **Exercise 5: Listing:** List the 20 goals under the three headings above. The secret is to write the three headings, then add the sub-headings under each section. Then write for 10 minutes, use your imagination, focus on the heading and let your pen do the work.*

***Refer to paragraph 4.5 on page 47** - **Exercise 6: Goal Notation:** You now have a written "goal notation". Now, for each goal mark a "timeline" of achievement, viz: 1 month, 6 months, 12 months, 18 months and 2 years. Now, for each "timeline" add two review dates. Finally print out the "goal notation" and for each goal write "why" you want to achieve success.*

Interstellar spacecraft WoW is now departing from Chapter 4 "The Supremacy of Goal Setting" and is on route to Chapter 5 "The Critical Seventeen "Cs"".

"….Please take your seats and fasten your seat belts.

The WoW will be travelling at the speed of light and will arrive at Chapter 5 "The Critical Seventeen "Cs"" in about 5 minutes…."

CHAPTER 5

Interstellar spacecraft WoW will be arriving at....

The Critical Seventeen "Cs"

I hope you found your visit to "The Supremacy of Goal Setting" both enlightening and life changing. To review, Exercises 1 to 6 should be completed in your journal and you should have your goals clearly written. The three final stipulations to goal setting are:

1. Highlight your top three short-term goals.
2. Do something now that will commence the journey of achievement – a telephone call, research, revise the action plan, take advice, find a role model who has achieved the same goal.
3. Read your goals every day.

The Critical Seventeen "Cs"....

From the employee to the employer - the Critical Seventeen "Cs" that, if scrutinised, will change you.

> *"Professionalism is a frame of mind, not a pay cheque".*
> *Cecil Castle.*

"The Supremacy of Goal Setting" behind us, I hope you appreciated the personal benefit of goal setting and have completed Exercises 5 and 6.

So now take your seats, we are arriving at a clever use of the letter "C".

Chapter 5 is about the Critical Seventeen "Cs"

5.1   Prerequisite.
5.2   These are your Critical Seventeen "Cs".
5.3   Advice for Improving Personal "Cs".
5.4   Exercise 7: List the "Cs".
5.5   Exercise 8: Summary.
5.6   The Challenge.

5.1   Prerequisite:

The S.W.O.T. is strengths, weaknesses, opportunities and threats. As a prerequisite to the Critical Seventeen "Cs", the S.W.O.T. {refer to Chapter 9 "The S.W.O.T." on page 79} test should have assisted in identifying at least some areas of your personal development that can be improved.

For clarity, you can refer to Chapter 9 "The S.W.O.T." on page 79 now!

Remember: It is essential to always be positive about your strengths, while at the same time looking to see how you can negate or eliminate your weaknesses. Similarly, use any opportunities to your advantage and try to lessen the effects of any threats. In any person or employer, there are always certain skills which need working on, or new skills that need to be acquired. The skills people used to talk about were the 3 R's - reading, writing and 'rithmetic. These skills are still useful, but there are just as many other skills that are as important or more important and are often called 'soft skills'. Coincidentally many of them begin with the letter "C".

5.2   These are your Critical Seventeen "Cs"

1.0   Calculating: Meaning the capability to perform calculations, especially arithmetical calculations, a calculating machine.

However, the calculating entrepreneur {the activity of setting up a business or businesses, taking on financial risks in the hope of profit: an entrepreneur is a problem solver} is both shrewd and cautious, a wise and calculating person.

2.0 **Calm:** Mentally, nearly or completely motionless; undisturbed: the calm surface of the lake. Not excited or agitated; composed viz:

> *"the leader was calm throughout the business crisis".*

3.0 **Camaraderie:** Mutual trust and friendship among people who spend a lot of time together "the enforced camaraderie of office life".

4.0 **Caring:** A state of mind in which one looks after or is concerned with another's well-being.

5.0 **Charisma:** A spiritual power or personal quality that gives an individual influence or authority over a large number of people.

6.0 **Charm:** The power of pleasing or attracting, as through personality or beauty, charm or manner:

> *"the charm of a mountain lake".*

7.0 **Cleanliness:** Personally neat; careful to keep or make clean:

> *"the cat is by nature a clean animal".*

8.0 **Coaching:** Coaching is training or development in which a person called "a coach" supports a learner in achieving a specific personal or professional goal.

9.0 **Command:** Give an authoritative or peremptory order.

10.0 **Commitment:** The state or quality of being dedicated to a cause, activity, etc.

11.0 **Communication:** The imparting or exchanging of information by speaking, writing or using some other medium.

12.0 **Comprehension:** The ability to understand something:

> *"some will not have the least comprehension of what I am trying to do".*

13.0 **Computing:** The use or operation of computers.

14.0 Concentration: The action or power of focusing all of one's attention.

"she was frowning in concentration".

15.0 Courage: Bravery, the ability to do something that frightens one:

"she called on all her courage to face the ordeal".

16.0 Courteous: Polite, respectful or considerate in manner.

17.0 Culture: The arts and other manifestations of human intellectual achievement regarded collectively.

All these 'Cs' are of some use in day-to-day life, be it whilst at work, or within a social environment that they become development tools.

By applying the "Cs" to your character and personality you have a good starting base for feeling positive about yourself if you are not too confident, at the same time highlighting some areas for improvement,

If you wonder where you can improve, everyone has their own particular skills, it is just a matter of identifying them and learning how to use them.

Take "charm" for instance, you only need to think of how much success James Bond has had, both on film and in box office sales, to see how highly charm is rated. Just think, with a little more suave sophistication, you could be the next Sean Connery.

This is my essential guide to some of the "Cs" in action and, more importantly, how they can help you. If you think that some of them appear a bit basic, just remember how many times you have come across people making basic errors in life.

5.3 Advice for Improving Personal "Cs"

Scampi for tea {take the first letter of each {SCAMPI} to form the six paragraphs below}:

Sociability: Get to know as many people as possible: the more people you know, the more opportunities you will hear about. Networking might sound odious, but it never hurts to have friends in high or useful places.

Clock-watching: Do not be a clock-watcher. If you have finished your task, ask what else you can do. Better still, do something useful without being asked. It might sound idealistic but over time it will be noticed and earning yourself a reputation as "a doer" may well open doors in the future.

Appearance: Be smart in appearance. Dress appropriately for interviews and always try to dress at least as smartly as your colleagues in your workplace. Take pride in your appearance and personal hygiene, like it or not people make instant judgements all the time so if you do not look {or smell} the part, you are fighting a losing battle. If work-mates invite you out, do make the effort to go occasionally, even if you are not a social animal and the office workers collectively have the manners of Attila the Hun.

Manners: Good manners make men and women. This applies just as much when you are writing letters, as to when you are speaking. Smile, shake hands and ask 'how are you?' use 'please' and 'thank you'. It might seem obvious, but do you always do this? Also, a misspelled letter looks unprofessional, always proofread and spell check. If someone asks for something, make YES your instinctive reaction.

Be a 'CAN-DO' person.

Punctuality: Do not be late for starting work, appointments, interviews etc. It is better to be 15 minutes early than 15 minutes late, it will not kill you and, as an added bonus, it gives you the opportunity to compose yourself and collect your thoughts on the task in hand.

Interest: Take an interest in everything that goes on around you, not just your own task; that way you will learn much more and also develop transferable skills which are likely to be appreciated by others.

"No one likes undue negativity and, remember, that glass really is half full".

Civil Pilots Training Program {take the first letters of each word – CPTP – to form the three paragraphs below}:

Criticism: Do not criticise others. Never gossip or backstab. It may be very tempting sometimes, but just remember that you would not like people talking about you behind your back.

Praise: Do not expect praise and recognition for everything you do. Do your best for yourself, not just because you think someone else is watching. It is always nice to get recognition, but learn to take pride in your own work and to see that as an ample reward, anything else is a bonus.

Team Player: Be a team player. If you can see someone else is busy, offer to help.

So here we are at the end of the Critical Seventeen "Cs" chapter, now for the exercises.

5.4 **Exercise 7: List the "Cs":** List the Critical Seventeen "Cs" and rate each "C" from 1 to 10. If the "C" strongly represents your self-opinion, your rate will be nearer 10 than 0, conversely, if the "C" does not represent your self-opinion and improvement in this area would be beneficial, your rate will be nearer 0 than 10. Then, re-read paragraph 5.3. {Advice for improving personal "Cs"} and again rate yourself from 0 to 10 using the method described above.

5.5 **Exercise 8: Summary:** This exercise requires you to summarise yourself from the data collated in Exercise 7 above and to compile two essays viz how you would describe yourself and then how you would describe the person you want to become. A very powerful exercise.

5.6 **The Challenge:** Exercises 7 and 8 are involved and time consuming. So, the challenge is to complete both exercises and then trust someone to read through them and pass comment. Then you should commence on an improvement programme that you must review at monthly intervals.

**Interstellar spacecraft WoW is now departing
from Chapter 5 "The Critical Seventeen "Cs""
and is on its way to Chapter 6 "People".**

"….Please take your seats and fasten your seat belts.

The WoW will be travelling at the speed of light and will arrive at Chapter 6 "People" in about 5 minutes…."

CHAPTER 6

Interstellar spacecraft WoW will be arriving at....

People

Welcome to Chapter 6 "People". Chapter 5 "The Critical Seventeen "Cs"" is a wonderful self-realisation tool and I hope you read and understood the meanings. Trusting you to have completed Exercises 7 and 8, we now launch into an absorbing subject which I call "People".

> *You can buy a person's hands but you cannot buy his heart.*
> *His heart is where his enthusiasm, his loyalty is.*
> *Stephen Covey.*

People - employees are the life force of all businesses. Employee recruitment is a transaction of the relationship between an organisation and its employees.

An "engaged employee" is one who is fully absorbed by and enthusiastic about their work and so takes positive action to further the organisation's reputation and interests.

Chapter 6 "People" is about:

6.1   The Peter Principle.
6.2   Top-rated Employees.
6.3   Exercise 9: 10 point self-rating.
6.4   Exercise 10: The Self Improvement Plan.
6.5   The Challenge.

An organisation with 'high' employee engagement might, therefore, be expected to outperform those with 'low' employee engagement, all else being equal. There are, however, a range of definitions that have emerged around concepts relating to employee engagement.

Research has looked at the involvement, commitment and productivity of employees. Organisations have often had a focus on how to generate engagement, rather than seeking objective ways to measure it. Care must, therefore, be taken when looking at some of the statistics presented around engagement.

6.1   The Peter Principle:

What is the 'Peter Principle'? The Peter Principle was first perceived by Dr. Laurence J. Peter published in his book, "The Peter Principle", in 1968.

The Peter Principle is an observation that, in an organisational hierarchy, every employee will rise or get promoted to his or her level of incompetence.

The Peter Principle is based on the notion that employees will get promoted as long as they are competent, but at some point will fail to get promoted beyond a certain job because it has become too challenging for them. Employees rise to their level of incompetence and stay there. Over time, every position in the hierarchy will be filled by someone who is not competent enough to carry out his or her new duties.

6.2   Top-rated employees:

The concept of working for money not service is a credo, which is a statement of the belief or purpose which guides someone's actions. Top-rated employees reverse this paradigm, viz – provide an exceptional service and a higher reward follows. There are eight qualities of remarkable employees that I have compiled over the years:

1. **Great and remarkable employees follow processes:** Some employees buck the systems and are constantly interfering with the status quo: reworking a timeline, adjusting a process, modifying a workflow.

   Great employees follow processes. Remarkable employees find ways to make those processes even better, not only because they are expected to, but because they just cannot help it.

2. **Ignore job descriptions:** Great employees are flexible and disregard job descriptions. The smaller the company, the more important it is that employees can think on their feet, adapt quickly to shifting priorities and do whatever it takes, regardless of role or position, to get things done.

When a key customer's project is in jeopardy, remarkable employees know without being told when there is a problem and they jump in without being asked, even if it's not their job.

3. **Recognition of contribution**: The most remarkable employees recognise the contribution of others, especially in group settings where the impact of their words is even greater.

4. **Different:** The best employees are often different, unusual, sometimes cheeky, even delighting in being unusual. They seem slightly odd, but in a really good way. Unusual personalities shake things up, make work more fun and transform ordinary teams into extraordinary teams simply by their presence.

   People who are not afraid to be different naturally stretch boundaries and challenge the status quo, they also often come up with the best ideas.

5. **Play and serious:** Remarkable employees know when to play and when to be serious, when to be irreverent and when to conform, when to challenge and when to back off. It is a tough balance to strike, but a rare few can walk that fine line with ease.

6. **Forward thinking:** We all want employees to bring issues forward, but some problems are better handled in private. Great employees often get more latitude to bring up controversial subjects in a group setting, because their performance allows greater freedom. Remarkable employees come to you before or after a meeting to discuss a sensitive issue, knowing that bringing it up in a group setting could cause tension.

7. **Showing who is wrong:** Good employees get satisfaction when proving others wrong. Self-motivation often comes from a desire to show that doubters are mistaken. The employee without a degree, or the one who was told they did not have leadership potential, often possess a burning desire to prove other people wrong.

   Education, intelligence, talent and skill are important, but drive is critical. Remarkable employees are driven by something deeper and more personal than just the desire to do a good job.

8. **Confidence to speak:** Good employees will speak up when others will not. Some employees are hesitant to speak up in meetings. Some are even hesitant to speak up privately. An employee once asked me a question about potential layoffs. After the meeting I said to him:

"Why did you ask about that? You already know what's going on."

He replied,

"I do, but a lot of other people don't and they're afraid to ask. I thought it would help if they heard the answer from you."

Remarkable employees have an innate feel for the issues and concerns of those around them and step up to ask questions or raise important issues when others hesitate.

6.3 **Exercise 9: 10 point self-rating:** If you are an employee, rate yourself under the following headings. If you are an employer, rate your best employee under the same headings:

1. Appearance.
2. Cooperation.
3. Good communication skills.
4. Team player.
5. Politeness.
6. Honesty.
7. Helper of others.
8. Conscientious worker.
9. Time flexible and punctual.
10. Good constant job performance.

6.4 **Exercise 10: The Self Improvement Plan:** On a separate sheet of paper, list your five lowest score topics.

Employees - create a self-improvement program.

Employers - create and present a staff development process.

6.5 **The Challenge:** The challenge, if you are an employee, is to ask a person who you know to mark you out of 10 points on items 1-10 above, viz - eight qualities of remarkable employees.

If you are an employer, compile and print out the eight qualities and commence an employee self-appraisal scheme, refer to pages 60 to 61.

Interstellar spacecraft WoW is now departing from Chapter 6 "People" and is on course for Chapter 7 "Write a Book".

"….Please take your seats and fasten your seat belts.

The WoW will be travelling at the speed of light and will arrive at Chapter 7 "Write a Book" in about 5 minutes…."

CHAPTER 7

Interstellar spacecraft WoW will be arriving at....

Write a Book

Welcome to "Write a Book", I am sure you will find this chapter thought-provoking. This chapter is what I refer to as "the stand out in a crowd" principle. Before we start, how did you enjoy the last chapter, "People"? I trust you completed your exercises. Your journal must be looking "well used" and nearly full? You may need a second journal. I always remember a phrase I wrote in my own journal, I think it originated from the great Tony Robbins:

> *"If a life is worth living it's worth recording. To know where you are and were in business development – write it down and read it often".*

So, write a book, let me explain:

"The new business card is a published book".

An ambitious title, "Write a Book", so what do I mean? When we meet a prospective client, there are three elements of impression that rates or ranks us and the services we offer compared to other providers, the three elements are:

1. How you look.
2. What you say.
3. What you leave with them.

We discussed {1} how you look {refer to paragraph 1.4 {Exercise 1: Image Dressing} on page 28}, in this chapter, we concentrate on {2} what you say and {3} what you leave with them.

Chapter 7 "Write a Book" is about:

7.1   What you say.
7.2   What you leave with the prospective client.
        7.2a   The Business Card.
        7.2b   What you leave with them – your book.
7.3   Exercise 11: Write your elevator speech and learn it by heart.
7.4   Exercise 12: Write a contents page for your book.
7.5   Exercise 13: Design your new business card.
7.6   The Challenge.

7.1   What you say:

Based on the "elevator speech" theory, just like any good speech, the elevator speech should be opened with a hook to capture the listener's attention. It takes approximately two minutes for an elevator to move from the ground floor to the top floor, you have a captive audience, a prospective client's attention, for two whole minutes - what do you say?

My elevator speeches were written and learned 20 years ago and still hold good today in 2015.

My elevator speech number 1:

…."Hello {sir/madam/mr/mrs/ms}, I am David Wright, Principal of the David Wright Group, I have been keen to get in touch with you. Our registered Practice specialises in quality assurance, health and safety law and human resources. *I wanted to talk to you about our recognised approach to accredited quality assurances, particularly the new 2015 standard. I think it would be of benefit to you and your company. There is no professional fee charged for our advisory QA service. I have written a number of books on this subject, which I would value sharing with you.*

As a fellow of the institution, I am regarded as an "expert" in QA core skill. Can we exchange business cards? Or can I write down your contact details? This is my business card and please accept a copy of my Firm's "Professional Portfolio" book, I'm sure you will find it relevant to your company's scope of activities. I know you are busy, so is it OK if my secretary contacts you for an appointment? I can come to your office, or can you find time for a trip to our office and enjoy our corporate hospitality, or we could simply meet up for a coffee at "do dares" [see note 1]*, I have heard they do a great flat white……"*

Note 1: Always research to source a good coffee shop near the prospective client's office. Research, ask people "is that a good coffee shop?". You can use {and adapt} your elevator speech at a meeting, on the telephone and, the greatest of all, at a chance meeting.

I need three elevator speeches, here are speeches 2 and 3:

My elevator speech number 2:

…."Hello {sir/madam/mr/mrs/ms}, I am David Wright, Principal of the David Wright Group, I have been keen to get in touch with you. Our registered Practice specialises in quality assurance, health and safety law and human resources. *I wanted to talk to you about the benefits of joining our registered health and safety law firm. I am a fellow of the institution of paralegals and I am registered with the health and safety executive. We provide a documentation compilation and compliance service and indemnity insurance in the event of a fee for intervention imposed by the HSE. I think it would be of benefit to you and your company. There is no professional fee charged for our advisory health and safety law service. I have a published book titled "The Health and Safety Mentor", please accept this signed complimentary copy.*

My elevator speech number 3:

…."Hello {sir/madam/mr/mrs/ms}, I am David Wright, Principal of the David Wright Group, I have been keen to get touch with you. Our registered Practice specialises in quality assurance, health and safety law and human resources.

I wanted to talk to you about the benefits of joining our employment law service called the human resource mentor. In consultation and in compliance with ACAS we compile human resources documentation and publish a monthly employment law journal. There is no professional fee charged for our advisory employment law service. Can we exchange business cards? Or can I write down your contact details?

This is my business card and please accept a copy of this month's human resources journal, plus a copy of my Firm's "Professional Portfolio" book.

I'm sure you will find both books relevant to your company's scope of activities.

I know you are busy, so is it OK if my secretary contacts you for an appointment? I can come to your office, or you can have a trip to ours and enjoy our corporate hospitality, or we could simply meet up for a coffee at "do dares" [see note1] *I have heard they do a great flat white……"*

7.2   What you leave with the prospective client.

The answer to "what you leave with the prospective client" is two valuable items, your business card and your book.

7.2a   The Business Card. Without explanation, at a personal development event a speaker passed a tray around and asked all delegates to place their business cards face up on the tray. All complied in wonderment. Then the loaded tray was passed around and we were asked to scan the tray and the cards on there. All complied in wonderment. Next, we were asked to choose one card and write down as much information as we could recall from that card.

We were then asked to hand in our completed description sheets one by one, all delegates were asked to describe their chosen business card.

To my amazement, one card was described 8 times from amongst 20 delegates. Whose card was it? The speaker's of course. Was this a trick? No, this was a business idea and I wanted to know more about it.

> *"Great minds discuss ideas, average minds discuss events,*
> *and small minds discuss people".*
> *Eleanor Roosevelt.*

Here is the exercise in full: Imagine 50 business cards uniformly displayed on a table top. You see all the different colours, some you can read at a distance and others are clearly the £5.00 per 100 quality and so on. The professional business card is "Manna from Heaven", it speaks volumes and it says "this guy {gal} is a professional". The eyes of the lookers-on at the table are drawn, like a magnet to steel, to your business card. When I learned the above at the personal development event, it was like a light bulb switching on, this presenter knew his stuff.

After the event, I discarded all of my business cards and paid a fee to have my new business card designed.

The WoW Business Card: A good business card projects your importance and professionalism. A good business card is printed on both sides and displays the following:

1. **Your name:** Clear and formal: showing your title and post nominal letters plus any designations.
2. **Telephone number:** Land line and mobile. Never just a mobile number. Consider having a call-forward facility installed, then you can display a main land line number only on your new business card.
3. **Email/web address:** Display as near to your name as possible.
4. **Your photograph:** Passport size, but use a professional photographer. Dress in your professional style, as if you were visiting a client. The professional passport size photograph must show head and shoulders only.
5. **What you do:** A précis of what you do in the least number of words as possible.
6. **Badges and logos.** Display logos of institutes, trade associations you subscribe to and finally design, or have designed for you, your initials or company in a very distinct logo.

Define a primary colour, a background colour and a distinct font. I now use the table top card exercise when presenting a development seminar, I am always in the top two card choices.

Finally on this topic, when presenting or placing your new business card, always give or lay the card photograph side up. Graphics and photos attract the eyes, words do not. Be like an actor rehearsing the presentation of your business card.

I knew a very successful consultant who rotated his business card in his fingers as he was talking, then when he had the attention of the listener presented his card.

7.2b **What you leave with them – your book**. Now, the chapter is titled "Write a Book". In this chapter, we have discussed elevator speeches and business cards, all vitally important elements, but not the real passport to the WoW Factor, which is presenting your book with your business card. I am a published author and have a passion for writing. You, the WoW Factor business guru, need a simple, professionally prepared, published and printed profile type book. Here is how you do it.

"A profile is a short article giving a description of a person or an organisation".

In the preparation of your professional portfolio covering the scope of your organisation, you need to include a few essentials as detailed below:

> Page 1 - What the publication is about:
> > "This is the professional profile of…."
> > "The organisation was founded…."
> > "We have been in business since…."
> > "Our scope of services include.…"

> Page 2 - About you. Your experience and qualifications, any unique features.

> Page 3 - Scope of services listed. Each service titled, explain any legal requirements, British Standards and your method of supplying this service. {Use a page per service}.

7.3   Exercise 11: Write your elevator speech and learn it by heart.

7.4   Exercise 12: Write a contents page for your book.

7.5   Exercise 13: Design your new business card.

7.6   The Challenge: I cannot over emphasise the importance of this chapter. The challenge is to write a book and produce a business card.

I presented this exercise at a mentoring seminar, some years ago. I was asked by a delegate if the business card and book was important for an individual who is furthering his or her career.

The answer is yes.

The book is your curriculum vitae {CV}, beautifully bound with a photograph. Your business card is your personal card, following the pattern of the advice above. Imagine a job interview, with your exclusive CV and personal card on the desk in front of the interviewer – will it stand out?

**Interstellar spacecraft WoW is now departing from
Chapter 7 "Write a Book" and will be arriving at
Chapter 8 "The Key to Successful Businesses".**

"….Please take your seats and fasten your seat belts.

The WoW will be travelling at the speed of light and will arrive at Chapter 8 "The Key to Successful Businesses" in about 20 minutes…."

CHAPTER 8

Interstellar spacecraft WoW will be arriving at....

The Key to Successful Businesses

Is there, or is there not, a key to business success? I remember, many years ago, a long established client asking me how I had managed to survive so long in business. I dwelled on this question long and hard. How had I lasted so long {probably 20 years} when many businesses are so short lived? After long deliberation, I finalised on six key traits that I have developed and practised for years, which are shared in similar form by successful business people.

Before we start this journey, did you complete the exercises in Chapter 6 "People"? Let me ask you a question. So far you have been presented with 13 exercises to complete. How many have you completed?

> *"Procrastination is one of the most common and deadliest of*
> *diseases and its toll on success and happiness is heavy".*
> *Wayne Dyer.*

Remember: you can obtain "The WoW Factor" as a training course or a talking book available from our Book Shop:

www.davidwrightservices.co.uk

So, the key to business success exists and here is my explanation.

Chapter 8 "The Key to Successful Businesses" is about:

8.1   My six point credo.
8.2   Success leaves clues.

8.1   My six point credo:

Credo 1: Take responsibility.

You are totally responsible for your life. This is the fundamental principle that you must embrace if you plan to have happiness and success in life and work.

I coached a young woman circa 10 years ago, she was a manager in a small company. I was struck, every time we met, by her failure to take responsibility for what was happening in her work and life.

"Everything is someone else's fault".

Every problem was explained away with reasons about why she could not affect the situation or the outcome.

You must take responsibility.

Credo 2: Do what you say.

A very simple principle to adopt.
My clients know that:
> If I say I will, I will do it.
> If I say I will contact on, say, Wednesday, I will.
> If I say "your job will be completed by", it is.

Credo 3: The power of goal setting.

Remarkable - read Chapter 4 "The Supremacy of Goal Setting" on page 43. Goal setting is possibly the ultimate commencement of personal and business development.

Credo 4: Be an optimist.

I love these explanations:

The optimist – believes in the glass is always half full principle.

The optimist – is a happy person.

The optimist – is a lucky person.

The optimist – believes that positive thinking improves work performance.

The optimist – has a balanced life.

The optimist – is more successful professionally and financially.

Credo 5: You can learn anything you want.

You can learn anything you want, from a sport, a foreign language, a skill set, anything at all – all that is needed are three elements:

Element 1 – a burning desire.

Refer to the Earl Nightingale saying above

"We become what we think about".

Element 2 – a written plan.

Write a plan.

This also has three elements:

1. Describe in detail what you want to learn - {what}.
2. Who can help? Is there a book? A course? A role model – {how}.
3. Keep a diary.

Element 3 – a flexible approach.

Constantly review, if it is not working, try something else – but always update your plan along the journey to accomplishment.

Never give in.

Credo 6: Learn from everyone you meet.

"I have worked for, and with, hundreds of companies and individuals and have had the privilege and pleasure of working with, and learning from, many top, successful professional

business movers and shakers. Opposing this, I have met many what I term "business vagabonds", both male and female, who milk the very life blood out of their clients and staff.

They cheat and lie, are without scruples to earn a pound, all at the expense of others. Needless to say, I did not work for these miscreants for long but learned from them the valuable lesson of the types of business people to avoid". Learn!

8.2   Success leaves clues.

Clue 1   Blame and excuses are the hallmarks of an unsuccessful life.

On television, I briefly watched three jailed individuals, who are seeking parole from the Parole Board, talking about themselves. I noticed the same pattern in their reasoning and approach to life. Nothing was their fault, including the incidents that landed each of them in jail.

I suspect that if I interviewed more incarcerated individuals, I would find a pattern of "not my fault." That is why taking responsibility for choices, actions and direction is so powerfully important.

Without taking responsibility, you will likely look at your life as a failure, because you allowed yourself to be blown "hither and yon" by any passing wind, then blame the wind for how things turned out.

Clue 2   Complete responsibility.

People who take complete responsibility for their lives experience joy and control of circumstances. They are able to make choices because they understand that they are responsible for their choices. Indeed, even when events that are not under your control go awry, you can, at least, determine how you will react to the event. You can make an event a disaster or you can use it as an opportunity to learn.

No matter how hard you try to blame others for events in your life, each event is the result of choices you have made and are making.

Clue 3   The little voice in your head.

Listen to the little voice in your head. Observe yourself talking with co-workers, family members and friends. Do you hear yourself taking responsibility or placing blame? Listen to the voice in your head. Eliminate blame; eliminate excuses. If the blame track, or the excuse track, plays repeatedly in your mind, you are shifting responsibility for your decisions and life to others.

Clue 4   Listen to yourself.

Listen to yourself when you speak. In conversation, do you hear yourself blame others for things that do not go exactly as you want? Do you find yourself pointing fingers at your co-workers or your upbringing, your parents, influenced by the amount of money that you make, or your spouse? Are you making excuses for goals unmet or tasks that have missed their deadlines? If you can hear your blaming patterns, you can stop them.

Clue 5   Feedback.

If an individual you respect supplies feedback that you make excuses and blame others for your woes, take that feedback seriously. Control your defensive reaction, explore examples and deepen your understanding with the co-worker or friend. People who responsibly consider feedback attract much more feedback.

8.3   Exercise 14: Six role model traits to copy or avoid:

Name 6 people who you can learn from. Under each name write:
    What do I admire about this person?
    What do I loathe about this person?
    What can I emulate from this person?
    What trait can I avoid adopting about this person?

8.4   Exercise 15: Five clues:

Study the 5 clues above and write an informative essay for each clue, as it applies to you.

8.5   The Challenge: The challenge is to simply re-read your journal and the 15 completed exercises.

Can you do it? – I know you can.

**Interstellar spacecraft WoW is now departing from
Chapter 8 "The Key to Successful Businesses"- we
are heading for Chapter 9 "The S.W.O.T." shortly.**

"….Please take your seats and fasten your seat belts.

The WoW will be travelling at the speed of light and will arrive at Chapter 9 "The S.W.O.T." in about 20 minutes…."

CHAPTER 9

Interstellar spacecraft WoW will be arriving at....

The S.W.O.T.

The Strengths, Weaknesses, Opportunities and Threats

No, not Special Weapons and Tactics, but Strengths, Weaknesses, Opportunities and Threats.

How did you find Chapter 8 "The Key to Successful Businesses"?

A tension breaker.

I remember presenting an after dinner speech on motivation. There were two speakers and I was on second after dinner. The first speaker was from Hartlepool, my home town, I had not met him previously but after a brief chat – I liked him. I never use jokes in a presentation, he did. A joke which I and the audience appreciated was:

> *"Sorry I am late. The police had the town centre cordoned off because they were investigating a suspicious object in a car. All's well, it turned out to be a tax disc".*

I went on and for the first time ever told a joke, I said:

> *"Sorry I'm late, I found a tax disc in the town centre and did not know what it was, so I put it in my car and caused chaos".*

Back to work:

Regardless of whether you are the employer or the employee, in order to work at your best, it is important that you know about yourself.

Chapter 9 "The S.W.O.T." is about:

9.1   The S.W.O.T.
9.2   The S.W.O.T. Summary.
9.3   The S.W.O.T. Test for you.
9.4   Exercise 16: Complete the paragraph 9.3 S.W.O.T. test for yourself.
9.5   Exercise 17: Produce a list from your S.W.O.T.
9.6   The Challenge.

9.1   The S.W.O.T.

You need to know what you are good at and what you enjoy doing. As with any business, there will be individual strengths and weaknesses. In order to discover these, you need a system, and what better than to use the same system that companies use. A common test that companies use to check their strengths and weaknesses is the S.W.O.T. test. That is Strengths, Weaknesses, Opportunities and Threats. The company looks at all its functions, makes a list for each strength, weakness, opportunity and threat and commences a risk analysis.

Below is an imaginary S.W.O.T. test for a well-known celebrity. Have a look and see what you think; no doubt you could add a few more comments about him.

S.W.O.T. example {1} celebrity Wayne Rooney:

S.W.O.T.

Strengths	**Weaknesses**	**Opportunities**	**Threats**

Strengths	**Weaknesses**
Married fame and fortune	Unpopular
Very good looking	Strong temper
Good feet	Not always reliable
Member of an excellent team	
Very fit	

Opportunities	**Threats**
National career	Injury
Europe	Media hostility
Captaincy	Lack of alternative career

S.W.O.T. example {2} the author:

S.W.O.T.

Strengths	Weaknesses	Opportunities	Threats

Strengths	**Weaknesses**
Highly experienced in business	Outdated technology
30 years running the business	Limited human resources
Very reliable and honest	Online presence
Always does what he says	Branding and reputation
Has the WoW Factor	Marketing budget
Published author	

Opportunities	**Threats**
Increase turnover	Competitors
Expand to Europe	
Increase staffing	

9.2   The S.W.O.T. Summary.

In summary, the author has used the S.W.O.T. analysis to examine the strengths and weaknesses of the businesses and identify potential opportunities and threats. Uncovering these factors can help business owners and individuals focus on growing their businesses/themselves and attracting customers/potential employers. Weaknesses, as identified in the S.W.O.T. analysis, need "attention" for business and self-improvement.

Outdated Technology.

Today's business world relies on technology for everything from inventory management to communicating with customers. When a business uses outdated technology it can slow down productivity and contribute to the business losing money. For example, if a graphic design company uses a desktop publishing program that most printers do not use any more, it could limit the type of printer the company can work with and negatively impact on how files are formatted and transferred.

Human Resources.

Limited human resources is a weakness many small business owners discover they have when they do their S.W.O.T. analysis. Limited human resources can include having a small staff, which makes it difficult to tackle every item on the company's to-do list. On the other hand, a company with a full staff that lacks the skills and training necessary to perform tasks can be a hindrance.

If a company wants to launch its social media presence, but none of the staff has experience in social media, it can be a major weakness for the company. Either they will have to hire a consultant or risk an unsuccessful social media launch.

Branding and Reputation.

Small businesses have competitors that may have better branding and a better reputation than they themselves have. This type of weakness is prevalent when customers are already familiar with a specific store or brand and then a small business creates or offers a competing product or service. Companies with better brand recognition and established reputations see a higher percentage of the market share, which is a potential weakness for a small operation.

Marketing Budget.

Marketing is a key factor in promoting products and services to customers, whether through pay-per-click campaigns or by offering product samples to potential customers. If a business lacks the budget for marketing, this is a major weakness that can affect how much of the market share a business acquires and how high its sales are from quarter to quarter.

Now, try to complete a S.W.O.T. for yourself, being totally honest with yourself of course!

Remember:

Strengths and weaknesses: These are usually things internal to you - about your skills, personality, character, etc. For strengths they might be things you are good at or enjoy. Weaknesses are things you feel you are not good at, or do not enjoy.

Opportunities and threats: These might be about people you know, job openings that might occur and other external factors that might impact on your life.

For example, opportunities might be contacts you have in companies through friends or family, or maybe new companies opening in the area. Threats, on the other hand, might be losing your job or benefits, or perhaps competition from others {someone else getting the job you want}.

9.3   The S.W.O.T. Test for you.

S.W.O.T. test for you: *Photocopy this page and complete:*

Your name: *Date:*

S.W.O.T.

Strengths   **Weaknesses**   **Opportunities**   **Threats**

Strengths   **Weaknesses**

Opportunities   **Threats**

Doing a S.W.O.T. test for yourself is not always the easiest thing to do. It requires subjectivity and sometimes we can all be over-critical, or unaware of our pluses or minuses.

Non-Executive Directors {NED}: It is always good to seek advice and suggestions from those who know you and a NED is usually a great person to help. NED stands for Non-Executive Director and companies will often include NEDs on their Board of Directors to give them independent advice. NEDs can bring specialist expertise and guidance to young businesses that could not possibly have amassed such knowledge themselves. They are often well networked and can provide useful contacts. Your NEDs might be your family, friends or friends of family, but what is important is that they are people who know you well and whose opinion you respect. Take them out for a coffee, or even a beer, and discuss your S.W.O.T. test with them. After explaining the concept, ask them nicely if they would like to be a NED in your Me-unlimited Company. Hopefully they will be honoured to help. Your NED can offer you objective advice, may have useful contacts and may offer some extra ideas for you that you might not otherwise have considered.

9.4 **Exercise 16:** Complete paragraph 9.3 {S.W.O.T. test for you}.

9.5 **Exercise 17:** Produce a list from your S.W.O.T. of your strengths and weaknesses and find a NED for advice.

9.6 **The Challenge**: Produce an action plan to eradicate your weaknesses and enhance your strengths.

Interstellar spacecraft WoW is now departing from Chapter 9 "The S.W.O.T." and will be arriving Chapter 10 "The Secret" shortly.

"….Please take your seats and fasten your seat belts.

The WoW will be travelling at the speed of light and will arrive at Chapter 10 "The Secret" in about 20 minutes…."

CHAPTER 10

Interstellar spacecraft WoW will be arriving at….

The Secret

"Successfully building businesses"

Referring to Chapter 9 "The S.W.O.T.", as a Business Coach and Mentor it is very interesting for me to programme a number of S.W.O.T.s to measure individual development.

"I am often asked if I have found a secret – or at least a consistent answer to successfully building businesses over my career".

So on to Chapter 10 "The Secret". I have spent some time thinking about what characteristics so many of my successful business ventures share and, importantly, what went wrong when I did not get it right. Reflecting across 30 years, I have come up with four "secrets."

Chapter 10 "The Secret" is about:

10.1   Secret 1: Enjoy What You Are Doing.
10.2   Secret 2: Create Something That Stands Out.
10.3   Secret 3: Be a Good Leader.
10.4   Secret 4: Be Visible.
10.5   Exercise 18: A current business plan.
10.6   Exercise 19: A future business plan.
10.7   The Challenge.

10.1   Secret 1: Enjoy What You Are Doing.

Because starting a business is a huge amount of hard work, requiring a great deal of time, you had better enjoy it. I did not set out to build a business empire. I set out to create something I enjoyed that would pay the bills.

There was no great plan or strategy. One night some friends and I were chatting over a few drinks and decided to call our group "The David Wright Group", as we were all new to business. The name stuck and had a certain ring to it.

For me, building a business is all about doing something to be proud of, bringing talented people together and creating something that is going to make a real difference to other people's lives.

A businesswoman or a businessman is not unlike an artist. What you have when you start a company is a blank canvas; you have to fill it. Just as a good artist has to get every single detail right on that canvas, a businessman or businesswoman has to get every single little thing right when first setting up in business in order to succeed. However, unlike a work of art, the business is never finished, it constantly evolves.

If a business person sets out to make a real difference to other people's lives and achieves that, he or she will be able to pay the bills and have a successful business to boot.

10.2   Secret 2: Create Something That Stands Out.

Whether you have a product, a service or a brand, it is not easy to start a company and survive and thrive in the modern world. In fact, you have to do something radically different to make a mark today.

Look at the most successful businesses of the past 30 years. Microsoft, Google and Apple, for example, shook up a sector by doing something that had not ever been done before and by continually innovating. They are now among the dominant forces.

Create something that everybody who works for you is really proud of.

Businesses generally consist of a group of people and they are your biggest assets.

10.3   Secret 3: Be a Good Leader.

As a leader you have to be a really good listener. You need to know your own mind but there is no point in imposing your views on others without some debate. No one has a monopoly on good ideas or good advice.

Get out there, listen to people, draw people out and learn from them. As a leader you have also got to be extremely good at praising people.

Never openly criticise people, never lose your temper and always lavish praise on your colleagues for a job well done.

People flourish if they are praised. Usually they do not need to be told when they have done something wrong, because most of the time they already know it. If somebody is not working out, do not automatically throw him or her out of the company. A company should genuinely be a family. So see if there is another job within the company that suits them better. On most occasions you will find something for every single kind of personality.

10.4   Secret 4: Be Visible.

A good leader does not get stuck behind a desk. I have worked in an office, I have worked from home, but I get "out and about", meeting people. It seems I am travelling all the time but I always have a notebook in my back pocket to jot down questions, concerns or good ideas gleaned from meeting people.

When you are building a business from scratch, the key word for many years is "survival." It is tough to survive. In the beginning you have not got the time or energy to worry about saving the world. You have just got to fight to make sure you can look after your bank manager and be able to pay the bills. Literally, your full concentration has to be on surviving.

Obviously, if you do not survive, just remember that most businesses fail and the best lessons are usually learned from failure. You must not get too dispirited.

Just get back up and try again.

10.5 **Exercise 18: A current business plan**: Using the 4 secrets, write a business plan for your existing business. If you are an employee or a person looking for that special job, write a plan using the 4 secrets of the business you would like to work for in the future.

10.6 **Exercise 19: A future business plan**: Select a company or business you know and mark their performance against the 4 secrets.

10.7 **The Challenge**: The challenge is to write an essay against the 4 secrets as they affect you. How could you use the secrets to your advantage?

Interstellar spacecraft WoW is now departing from Chapter 10 "The Secret" and heading the long journey through time and space to planet Earth.

CHAPTER 11

Interstellar spacecraft WoW
Chapter 11 is an in-flight talk by David Wright about the Group.

About The David Wright Group

Good evening fellow passengers.

I am David Wright – the Author of "The WoW Factor". I am going to describe the Practice, "The David Wright Group" {"the Group"} and what we do. Our professional team of five operate the Group's activities in compliance with our registered and audited management systems. The Group, of which I am the Principal, awoke to the dawn of business enterprise and opportunity in 1985. We had the same management team from 1990 to 2006. The Group is registered to ISO 9001 {Quality Management System} and OHSAS 18001 {Occupational Health and Safety Management System}. The four sections of the business are described as follows:

Health and Safety:

Provision of a health and safety service, as prescribed under Regulation 7 of the Management of Health and Safety at Work Regulations 1999. Compilation of bespoke health and safety documentation.

Health and Safety Law:

Provision of a legal health and safety advice and representation service. Indemnity Insurance for Fee for Intervention via Wright's Health and Safety Law Firm and the International Institution of Risk and Safety Management {IIRSM} Fee for Intervention reimbursement scheme.

Human Resources:

Provision of service including preparation and amendment of Contracts of Employment, Grievance and Disciplinary Procedure and the provision of employment law guidance.

Quality Assurance:

Preparation of bespoke ISO 9001 2015 quality management systems, OHSAS 18001 health and safety management systems and ISO 14001 environmental management systems, for accreditation or registration.

Our Firm is a business podium, we do what we say; we keep in touch with our valued clients: we do a lot more than we charge a fee for.

Our associates/staff/clients/customers/suppliers and our competitors when discussing our business, say "WoW".

Our expertise, professionalism and qualifications in occupational health and safety, health and safety law, quality assurance and human resources, is evident not only by our 30 continuous, unbroken years in the business and our team of qualified staff and associates, but in the decades of satisfied clients who have come to expect nothing but the best.

"Captain – please return to your seats and prepare for landing".

CHAPTER 12

"The WoW Factor" final chapter

The Conclusion

Safely back to Earth after our epic voyage through
time and space, it is now time to reflect.

It is a rainy evening in Whickham and I have just "booted up" my computer and realised that I am starting my final chapter. If you are reading this chapter, I want to congratulate you for your endurance.

You know, most business people will not better themselves and their business, but their hopes, wishes and desires orbit their mind to rest in a place called "nowhere". They invest in consultants, buy into courses, invest in books, but take no action.

They say "one day?"

"The road to "one day" leads to a town called "nowhere"."
Tony Robbins.

The pathway to the WoW Factor is chartered in the chapters of this book. Even if you adopt just one idea written within this book, you move forward a giant step in front of your competitors.

We have enjoyed a new year's meal with friends. Well it is midnight, 31st December 2015, and we herald in the New Year of 2016, happy new year!

I'm home after a thirty minute drive, it is cold and I passed a few gritting wagons, but it was not too slippery.

So, did you walk my talk?

Did I exercise the WoW elements to stay in the WoW Factor? Have I taken my business to the next level and doubled my turnover?

I will tell you when we talk.

This is David Wright signing off.
dwac01@aol.com

CHAPTER 13

Index of Exercises

Similar to a worksheet, this is an index of all the exercises:

Chapter 1: The Clear Focus – page 25.

1.4 **Exercise 1: Image Dressing:** Image is the general impression that a person projects to the public. For this exercise, list the circumstances, venues and reasons that you come into contact with your clients and/or potential clients. Then describe your mode of dress. Do not just "think" this exercise – write it down and do it!

This exercise changed my business image. If after meeting delegates they cannot remember my name, they refer to me as the ….

> *"immaculately smart one with shiny shoes".*

To continue, the next part of presenting yourself, after appearance, is "what" you say and "how" you say it. When talking to your clients and/or potential clients, here are my top guideline points on the skill of conversing with them:

1. Speak quietly and slowly, do not raise your voice or shout. Be natural, practice fairly slow monologue in front of a mirror, using a newspaper or similar. Another good idea is to record a prose into a recording device, i.e. your iPhone. Practice, practice, and practice again, because repeated practice makes mastery.
2. Remove from your vocabulary words and phrases such as "didn't we" and "isn't it" etc. Such words and phrases are "yes tags" and are the habitually calling for the other person to say "yes".

3. Practice listening skills. A good conversation is 40% talking, 40% listening and 20% gentle silence.

The next part of "what" you say and "how" you say it, is to say the right things. What do I mean? I mean when talking to clients and/or potential clients, regarding current contracts or potential contracts.

Remember, these people are not your friends; they are the people who look at you to provide a professional service. When conversing you need to instil confidence by expressing your understanding of what they want, as well as your knowledge and experience to provide it. So, be able to explain yourself clearly, distinctly and succinctly.

Do what you say. Never exaggerate or make claims or promises that you cannot fulfil. Finally, master the art of listening. Listening involves not interrupting, hearing the spoken word and then interpreting the spoken words.

1.5 **Exercise 2: Speaking and Listening:** You have a meeting with a potential new client. Write a script, detailing your conversation with him. Write your introduction viz – *"I'm John Brown, the Principal of the Practice……"* followed by the details of the proposed contract, *viz – "from our initial conversation I understand….",* followed by your proposal, viz – *"what I propose, Mr Brown, is…."* and finally the closing viz – *"well Mr Brown, it was a pleasure to meet you, is there anything you want to ask me ????, I will compile a proposal for you and you will receive it next Wednesday, is that acceptable? ……"*

1.6 **The Challenge:** Here we are at the end of the first chapter of "The WoW Factor". The challenge is for you to complete the two exercises, before you continue your journey to the WoW Factor.

Chapter 2: Supporting CD-ROM – No exercises or challenge, information chapter only.

Chapter 3: Change Management – page 35.

3.6 **Exercise 3: Change Management {1}:** Define one major change that you are going to adopt into your business.

3.7 **Exercise 4: Change Management {2}:** Define your method of implementation and empower action. Define and state how to remove obstacles, enable constructive feedback and gain lots of support from leaders - reward and recognise progress and achievements. Refer to paragraph 3.8, Exercises 3 and 4 examples on page 39.

3.9 **The Challenge:** Here we are at the end of the third chapter, "Change Management". It is now time to compile paragraph 3.6 {Exercise 3: Change Management {1}} – page 39.

You will need to define one major change you are going to adopt into your business. It is also time to compose paragraph 3.7 {Exercise 4: Change Management {2}}. You will need to define your method of implementation and empower action. The challenge is extended to review Exercises 1 and 2 at the end of Chapter 1 "The Clear Focus".

Chapter 4: The Supremacy of Goal Setting - page 43.

4.4 **Exercise 5: Listing:** List 20 goals under the 3 headings above. The secret is to write the three headings, then add the sub-headings under each section. Then write for 10 minutes, use your imagination, focus on the heading and let your pen do the work.

4.5 **Exercise 6: Goal Notation:** You now have a written "goal notation". Now, for each goal, mark a "timeline" of achievement, viz: 1 month: 6 months: 12 months; 18 months and 2 years. Now, for each "timeline" add two review dates. Finally print out the "goal notation" and for each goal write "why" you want to achieve success.

Remember, the "why" is the driving force behind human behaviour. Find a big enough "why" and the "how" will follow. Imagine you have already achieved the individual goal.

Remember:
We become what we think about.

4.6 **The Challenge:** Here we are at the end of Chapter 4 "The Supremacy of Goal Setting". It is now time for the exercises. Complete Exercise 5 by writing 20 goals under the 3 headings. Then continue and complete Exercise 6, for the each goal mark a "timeline" of achievement.

The challenge is extended to review all exercises.

Refer to paragraph 1.4 on page 28 - Exercise 1: Image Dressing:

Image is the general impression that a person projects to the public. For this exercise, list the circumstances, venues and reasons that you come into contact with your clients and/or potential clients. Then describe your mode of dress. Do not just "think" this exercise – write it down and do it!

Hearing the spoken words, then interpreting the spoken words.

Refer to paragraph 1.5 on page 29 – Exercise 2: Speaking and Listening: *You have a meeting with a potential new client. Write script, detailing your conversation with him. Write your introduction viz – "I'm John Brown, the Principal of the Practice……" followed by the details of the proposed contract, viz – "from our initial conversation I understand….", followed by your proposal, viz – "what I propose, Mr Brown, is…." and finally the closing viz – "well Mr Brown, it was a pleasure to meet you, is there anything you want to ask me ????, I will compile a proposal for you, you will receive it next Wednesday, is that acceptable? ……"*

Refer to paragraph 3.6 on page 39 – Exercise 3: Change Management {1}: *Define one major change that you are going to adopt into your business.*

Refer to paragraph 3.7 on page 39 – Exercise 4: Change Management {2}: *Define your method of implementation and empower action. Define and state how to remove obstacles, enable constructive feedback and gain lots of support from leaders - reward and recognise progress and achievements.*

Refer to paragraph 4.4 on page 47 – Exercise 5: Listing: *List 20 goals under the 3 headings above. The secret is to write the 3 headings, then add the sub-headings under each section. Then write for 10 minutes, use your imagination, focus on the heading and let your pen do the work.*

Refer to paragraph 4.5 on page 47 – Exercise 6: Goal Notation: *You now have a written "goal notation". Now, for each goal mark a "timeline" of achievement, viz: 1 month: 6 months: 12 months; 18 months and 2 years. Now, for each "timeline" add two review dates. Finally print out the "goal notation" and for each goal write "why" you want to achieve success.*

Chapter 5: The Critical Seventeen "Cs" - page 51.

5.4   **Exercise 7: List the "Cs":** List the 17 "Cs" and rate each "C" from 1 to 10. If the "C" strongly represents your self-opinion, your rate will be nearer 10 than 0: Conversely, if the "C" does not represent your self-opinion and improvement in this area would be beneficial, your rate will be nearer 0 than 10. Then, re-read paragraph 5.3 {Advice for improving personal "Cs"} and again rate yourself from 0 to 10 using the method described above.

5.5   **Exercise 8: Summarise:** This exercise requires you to summarise yourself from the data collated in Exercise 7 above and to compile two essays viz how you would describe yourself and how you would describe the person you want to become. A very powerful exercise.

5.6 **The Challenge:** Exercises 7 and 8 are involved and time consuming. So, the challenge is to complete both exercises and then trust someone to read through them and pass a comment. Then you should commence on an improvement programme that you must review at monthly intervals.

Chapter 6: People - page 59.

6.3 **Exercise 9: 10 point self-rating:** If you are an employee rate yourself under the following headings. If you are an employer rate your best employee under the same headings:

1. Appearance.
2. Cooperation.
3. Good communication skills.
4. Team player.
5. Politeness.
6. Honesty.
7. Helper of others.
8. Conscientious worker.
9. Time flexible and punctual.
10. Good constant job performance.

6.4 **Exercise 10: The Self Improvement Plan:** On a separate sheet of paper, list your five lowest score topics.

Employees – create a self-improvement program.

Employers – create and present a staff development process.

6.5 **The Challenge:** The challenge, if you are an employee, is to ask a person who you know to mark you out of 10 points on item 1-10 above viz – eight qualities of remarkable employees.

If you are an employer, compile and print out the eight qualities and commence an employee self-appraisal scheme, refer to pages 60 to 61.

Chapter 7: Write a Book - page 65.

7.3   **Exercise 11:** Write your elevator speech and learn it by heart.

7.4   **Exercise 12**: Write a contents page for your book.

7.5   **Exercise 13**: Design your new business card.

7.6   **The Challenge:** I cannot over emphasise the importance of this chapter. The challenge is to write a book and produce a business card.

I presented this exercise at a mentoring seminar, some years ago. I was asked by a delegate if the business card and book was important for an individual who is furthering his or her career.

The answer is yes.

Write a contents page for your book.

Chapter 8: The Key to Successful Businesses - page 73.

8.3   **Exercise 14: Six role model traits to copy or avoid:**

Name 6 people who you can learn from. Under each name write:
What do I admire about this person?
What do I loathe about this person?
What can I emulate from this person?
What trait can I avoid adopting about this person?

8.4   **Exercise 15: Five clues:**

Study the 5 clues above and write an informative essay for each clue, as it applies to you.

8.5   **The Challenge:** The challenge is to simply re-read your journal and the 15 completed exercises.

Can you do it?

I know you can.

Chapter 9: The S.W.O.T. - page 79.

9.4   **Exercise 16:** Complete paragraph 9.3 {The S.W.O.T.}

9.5   **Exercise 17:** Produce a list from your S.W.O.T. of your strengths and weaknesses and find a NED for advice.

9.6   **The Challenge:** Produce an action plan to eradicate your weakness and enhance your strengths.

Chapter 10: The Secret - page 87.

10.5   **Exercise 18: A current business plan**: Using the 4 secrets, write a business plan for your existing business. If you are an employee or a person looking for that special job, write a plan using the 4 secrets of the business you would like to work for in the future.

10.6   **Exercise 19: A future business plan:** Select a company or business you know and mark their performance against the 4 secrets.

10.7   **The Challenge:** The challenge is to write an essay against the 4 secrets as they affect you. How could you use the secrets to your advantage?

To end, from where we started…

"In a world of change, the learners shall inherit the earth, while the learned shall find themselves perfectly suited for a world that no longer exists."

Eric Hoffer

Be a lifelong learner.

You did it, you finished the WoW Factor.
Congratulations.

David Wright signing off……

ABOUT THE AUTHOR

David Wright is a successful businessman, close to retirement. He is a well-educated management and executive consultant with over 30 experience behind him. He has two published books to his name, "The Health & Safety Mentor" and "Taking Charge". Born in the North East of England, he has worked in Europe and is well respected for his teachings and writings.

www.ingramcontent.com/pod-product-compliance
Lightning Source LLC
Chambersburg PA
CBHW081135170526
45165CB00008B/2684